A Note from the Author

To the dedicated professionals in the aviation industry who work tirelessly to ensure the safe and efficient operation of air traffic control and baggage handling systems. Your commitment to excellence inspires us all.

Introduction

"Air Traffic Control & Baggage Handling: A Kanban Story"

In today's fast-paced world, the efficient management of air traffic control and baggage handling systems is critical to the smooth operation of airports and airline services. As airlines strive to provide more reliable and efficient services to their customers, the need for effective management and optimisation of these complex systems is more important than ever.

This book dives into the application of Kanban principles in the context of air traffic control and baggage handling systems. Kanban, a proven method for managing and optimising workflow, has been widely adopted in various industries for its ability to streamline processes, reduce waste, and improve overall efficiency.

In this comprehensive guide, we will explore how Kanban can be applied to air traffic control and baggage handling systems to enhance operational efficiency, minimise delays, and ultimately improve the passenger experience. Through real-world case studies, practical examples, and expert insights, readers will gain a deep understanding of how Kanban principles can be tailored to suit the unique challenges and requirements of the aviation industry.

The book will cover a wide range of topics, including:

1. Applying Kanban to Air Traffic Control: An in-depth exploration of how Kanban can be implemented to optimise the management of air traffic control operations. From scheduling to resource allocation, this section will provide valuable insights into improving the efficiency and reliability of air traffic management.

2. Kanban in Baggage Handling Systems: A detailed examination of how Kanban principles can be leveraged to streamline the complex processes involved in baggage handling. Readers will learn how to minimise processing times, reduce errors, and enhance the overall performance of baggage handling systems.

3. Case Studies and Best Practices: Real-world case studies and best practices from leading airports and aviation organisations that have successfully implemented Kanban in their air traffic control and baggage handling systems. These insights will provide practical guidance and inspiration for organisations looking to embark on their own Kanban journey.

With its clear, practical approach and wealth of real-world examples, "Air Traffic Control & Baggage Handling: A Kanban Story" offers a valuable resource for aviation professionals, airport operators, airline executives, and anyone involved in the management of air traffic control and baggage handling systems. By mastering the principles of Kanban and applying them to these critical operational functions, organisations can unlock new levels of efficiency, reliability, and customer satisfaction in the dynamic world of aviation.

The Author

Julian Cambridge was born in London, UK.

- M.Sc. Business Computing
- B.Sc. (Hons) Computing with Business

Julian founded Golden Agile Solutions to supply IT consultancy activities to clients.

- Accredited Kanban Trainer (AKT, KMP, TKP)
- Certified Scrum Professional (CSM, CSPO, A-CSM, A-CSPO, CSP-SM)
- ICAgile Authorized Instructor (Agile Fundamentals, Agile Product Ownership, Agile Testing, Business Agility)

A Note from the Author..1
Introduction..2
The Author..5
Global Aviation System..7
Air Traffic Control..10
Air Traffic Control using Kanban......................................13
Air Traffic Control successful case studies....................16
Baggage Handling System..19
Baggage Handling System using Kanban.......................22
Real-time tracking for baggage using Kanban signals....26
Baggage Handling System successful case studies........31
Summary..34

Global Aviation System

The global aviation system encompasses the interconnected network of aviation activities, infrastructure, regulations, and organisations that facilitate air travel on a worldwide scale. This expansive system plays a pivotal role in enabling the movement of people and goods across international boundaries, connecting distant locations, and supporting economic growth and international trade. The following are key components and aspects of the global aviation system:

1. Air Transportation Network: The global aviation system consists of a vast network of airports, air traffic control facilities, and air routes that enable the movement of aircraft worldwide. This network facilitates scheduled passenger flights, cargo transport, and general aviation activities, providing essential links between cities, countries, and continents.

2. Airlines: Commercial airlines are central to the global aviation system, operating fleets of aircraft to transport passengers and cargo across domestic and international routes. These carriers are responsible for providing air transportation services, maintaining safety standards, and complying with international regulations.

3. Aircraft Manufacturing and Technology: The global aviation system relies on advanced aircraft technologies

and innovations developed by leading manufacturers. Ongoing advancements in aircraft design, propulsion systems, avionics, and materials contribute to the safety, efficiency, and environmental sustainability of air travel.

4. Airports and Infrastructure: Airports serve as critical hubs within the global aviation system, providing facilities for aircraft operations, passenger services, cargo handling, and maintenance activities. Infrastructure investments, such as modernised runways, terminals, and air traffic control systems, support the efficient operation of airports and contribute to the overall capacity of the aviation network.

5. Air Traffic Management: The management of air traffic, including air traffic control services, airspace design, and navigation procedures, is essential to maintaining the safety and efficiency of the global aviation system. Coordination between air traffic control authorities and aviation stakeholders is crucial for managing air traffic flows and ensuring the orderly movement of aircraft.

6. Regulatory Framework: International and national regulatory bodies, such as the International Civil Aviation Organisation (ICAO) and the Federal Aviation Administration (FAA) in the United States, establish and enforce standards and regulations to ensure the safety,

security, and environmental sustainability of aviation operations. Regulatory oversight encompasses areas such as aircraft certification, pilot training, airworthiness standards, and aviation security protocols.

7. International Cooperation and Agreements: The global nature of aviation requires extensive international cooperation and agreements to harmonise safety standards, air traffic procedures, and market access for airlines. Bilateral and multilateral agreements between countries govern aspects such as air transport services, route rights, and aviation security protocols.

8. Economic Impact: The global aviation system has a substantial economic impact, supporting millions of jobs, fostering tourism, and facilitating international trade and commerce. The interconnectedness of the aviation industry with other sectors of the economy underscores its role as a driver of global economic activity.

In summary, the global aviation system is a complex and dynamic network that encompasses a wide array of stakeholders, technologies, and regulatory frameworks. Its far-reaching impact extends beyond transportation, shaping global connectivity, economic development, and cultural exchange on a profound scale.

Air Traffic Control

Air traffic control (ATC) is a critical component of the aviation industry, responsible for ensuring the safe and efficient movement of aircraft in the sky and on the ground. The primary goal of air traffic control is to prevent collisions between aircraft and to facilitate the orderly flow of air traffic, thereby enhancing safety and minimising delays. This complex and vital function is conducted by highly trained and skilled air traffic controllers who work in various capacities at airports, area control centres, and radar facilities.

At airports, air traffic controllers stationed in control towers are responsible for overseeing the movement of aircraft on the ground, particularly during takeoff, landing, and taxiing. They provide clearances to pilots, monitor runway activity, and coordinate the movement of aircraft to maintain safe distances and prevent conflicts. Additionally, they communicate critical information to pilots, such as wind conditions, runway status, and traffic advisories.

In en route airspace, air traffic control is managed by controllers working in area control centres. These controllers are tasked with ensuring the safe separation and efficient routing of aircraft as they travel through controlled airspace. Using radar, computer systems, and communication tools, they monitor the positions and movements of aircraft, provide navigational assistance, and coordinate the handoff of flights between different sectors of airspace as they transition through the airspace system.

Radar facilities play a crucial role in air traffic control by providing surveillance and tracking of aircraft across wide areas of airspace. Radar controllers use radar displays and other tools to monitor aircraft movements, provide instructions to pilots, and ensure the safe and orderly flow of traffic in their designated airspace sectors.

To carry out their duties effectively, air traffic controllers undergo rigorous training and certification to develop the necessary skills and knowledge. This includes learning about aviation regulations, navigation, aircraft performance, weather patterns, and emergency procedures. Controllers must also possess strong spatial awareness, excellent communication skills, and the ability to make quick, informed decisions, especially in high-pressure situations.

The importance of air traffic control cannot be overstated, as it is fundamental to maintaining the safety and efficiency of air travel. By coordinating the movements of thousands of aircraft each day, air traffic control contributes to the overall reliability and success of the global aviation system. Furthermore, air traffic controllers play a vital role in responding to emergencies, providing assistance to pilots, and ensuring the swift and safe resolution of unexpected incidents.

In conclusion, air traffic control is a cornerstone of modern aviation, and the dedicated professionals who work in this field are essential to the safe and orderly operation of the world's airspace. Through their expertise, vigilance, and commitment to safety, air traffic controllers contribute to the continued success of air travel as a vital mode of transportation.

Air Traffic Control using Kanban

Air traffic control using Kanban involves applying the principles of Kanban, a lean management methodology originally developed by Toyota, to illustrate how air traffic control processes can be visualised, managed, and optimised. In the context of air traffic control, Kanban can be used to represent the flow of aircraft, the allocation of resources, and the management of tasks and activities within the ATC system.

1. Visualising the Workflow: In the context of air traffic control, the workflow can be visualised as a series of stages or lanes representing different activities, such as ground movements, departure sequencing, en route management, and arrival sequencing. Each aircraft's journey through the airspace and airport can be represented as a card on the Kanban board, moving from one stage to the next as it progresses through the system.

2. Work in Progress (WIP) Limits: Applying WIP limits to air traffic control processes can help ensure that controllers do not become overloaded with too many simultaneous tasks. This can be represented by limiting the number of aircraft in specific stages of the process, such as the number of aircraft waiting for takeoff

clearance or the number of aircraft being sequenced for approach and landing.

3. Continuous Flow: Kanban emphasises the importance of maintaining a continuous flow of work. In air traffic control, this can be represented by ensuring that aircraft move steadily through the different stages of their journey, with the aim of minimising delays and maintaining safe separations. By visualising the flow of aircraft, controllers can identify bottlenecks and take action to optimise the overall flow of air traffic.

4. Feedback Loops: Kanban encourages the use of feedback loops to continuously improve processes. In air traffic control, feedback can be obtained from controllers, pilots, and other stakeholders to identify areas for improvement, such as optimising airspace utilisation, streamlining communication protocols, or refining departure and arrival procedures.

5. Flexibility and Adaptability: Kanban promotes flexibility and adaptability in response to changing conditions. In air traffic control, this can be represented by the ability to dynamically adjust the flow of air traffic in response to weather events, traffic congestion, or unexpected incidents. Visualising the status of aircraft on the Kanban board can help controllers make informed decisions to adapt to evolving conditions.

6. Collaborative Work: Kanban encourages collaboration and shared responsibility. In air traffic control, this can be represented by the coordination between different control centres, tower controllers, and radar facilities. Visualising the flow of aircraft and relevant information on a shared Kanban board can enhance communication and coordination among different units within the ATC system.

By applying the principles of Kanban to air traffic control, it becomes possible to create a visual representation of the flow of aircraft and associated tasks, enabling controllers to manage workloads, identify inefficiencies, and continuously improve the management of air traffic. This approach can help enhance situational awareness, optimise resource allocation, and contribute to the overall safety and efficiency of the air traffic control system.

Air Traffic Control successful case studies

Several case studies highlight successful implementations and advancements in air traffic control. Here are a few notable examples:

1. Remote Tower Operations (Multiple Locations): Remote tower operations represent a significant advancement in air traffic control. The concept allows air traffic services at one airport to be provided from a remote location using advanced technology. In Sweden, for instance, the first remote tower operation was successfully implemented at Örnsköldsvik Airport in 2015. Since then, several other airports in Sweden and around the world have adopted remote tower technology, enabling more efficient and cost-effective provision of air traffic services.

2. London Heathrow Airport (UK): London Heathrow Airport, one of the busiest airports in the world, has seen successful implementations of advanced air traffic control procedures and technologies. This includes the use of time-based separation (TBS) for arrivals, a system that allows

aircraft to follow each other more closely while maintaining safe separation. TBS has contributed to increased runway capacity and reduced delays at the airport.

3. New York Terminal Radar Approach Control (TRACON) Consolidation (USA): The consolidation and modernisation of air traffic control facilities can have a significant impact on airspace management. In the United States, the consolidation of New York's TRACON facilities in 2015 brought together the airspace management for three major airports—John F. Kennedy International, LaGuardia, and Newark Liberty International—resulting in improved efficiency, reduced complexity, and enhanced collaboration among controllers.

4. Free Route Airspace Implementation (Europe): Free Route Airspace (FRA) initiatives in Europe have aimed to streamline air traffic control procedures by allowing aircraft to fly more direct routes, reducing fuel consumption, emissions, and flight times. Successful implementations of FRA, such as those in the airspace managed by EUROCONTROL's Maastricht Upper Area Control Centre, have demonstrated the potential for substantial environmental and economic benefits.

5. Single European Sky ATM Research (SESAR) Program: The SESAR program is a collaborative initiative aimed at modernising and harmonising air traffic management across Europe. Through research and development efforts, SESAR has led to the successful demonstration of advanced technologies and procedures, including trajectory-based operations, improved automation, and enhanced communication and surveillance capabilities.

These case studies demonstrate how advancements in air traffic control technologies, procedures, and collaborative initiatives have contributed to increased efficiency, enhanced safety, and reduced environmental impact in the management of air traffic. By embracing innovation and working towards harmonisation and standardisation, the global aviation industry continues to make significant strides in optimising air traffic control operations.

Baggage Handling System

The baggage handling system is a critical component of airport operations that is responsible for the efficient and secure handling of passenger luggage and cargo. This system encompasses a series of processes, equipment, and technologies designed to transport checked baggage from the point of passenger check-in to the aircraft, and vice versa. Here are the key components and functions of an airport luggage system:

1. Baggage Drop-off and Check-in: Passengers deposit their checked baggage at the airport's check-in counters or self-service kiosks. At this stage, the luggage is tagged with a unique barcode or RFID (Radio-Frequency Identification) tag that contains information about the flight, destination, and passenger details.

2. Baggage Sorting: Once checked in, the luggage is sorted based on its destination and flight. Automated conveyor belts, sortation systems, and baggage handling software are used to route each bag to the appropriate terminal, flight, and ultimately to the correct aircraft.

3. Screening and Security: Baggage is subject to security screening to detect prohibited items and ensure the safety of air travel. Advanced screening technologies,

such as explosive detection systems (EDS) and computed tomography (CT) scanners, are used to examine the contents of each bag.

4. Baggage Transfer: For passengers with connecting flights, the luggage system facilitates the transfer of bags between different flights and aircraft. Baggage that needs to be transferred is routed through the airport's baggage handling facilities and transferred to the appropriate connecting flights.

5. Storage and Holding Area: Baggage that arrives at the airport before its corresponding flight is stored in holding areas within the airport's baggage handling facility. These areas are equipped with automated storage systems or manual handling processes to keep luggage organised and accessible.

6. Aircraft Loading and Unloading: Baggage is transported to the aircraft using conveyor belts, tugs, and other ground support equipment. At the aircraft, ground handling staff load the luggage into the cargo hold or baggage compartments using specialised loading equipment.

7. Arrival and Reclaim: Upon arrival at the destination airport, luggage is unloaded from the aircraft and transported to the baggage claim area. Passengers retrieve their checked bags from carousels or designated reclaim points. Baggage reconciliation

systems ensure that each passenger retrieves the correct luggage.

Key technologies used in modern airport luggage systems include conveyor belts, automated sortation systems, baggage tracking systems, RFID technology, baggage handling software, security screening equipment, and automated storage and retrieval systems.

Efficient and reliable baggage handling systems are essential for ensuring a positive passenger experience, minimising delays, and enhancing airport operations. Additionally, the proper handling and tracking of luggage contribute to aviation security, safety, and compliance with international aviation regulations.

Baggage Handling System using Kanban

Implementing a Kanban system in baggage handling offers numerous benefits by enhancing efficiency, reducing errors, and facilitating a smoother flow of baggage through the system. Kanban, a lean and visual management method, could be adapted to the baggage handling process within airports to optimise operations.

Here's a breakdown of how Kanban could be applied to a baggage handling system:

1. Visual Management: Kanban's emphasis on visualising workflow and processes would involve using visual signals to indicate the status of baggage and its movement through different stages of handling. Each baggage item could be assigned a unique Kanban card or digital tag containing essential information such as destination, flight number, and priority status. These visual cues would enable staff to quickly identify, track, and manage the movement of baggage within the system.

2. Limiting Work in Progress (WIP): Applying the principle of limiting work in progress, the baggage handling system can ensure that resources and capacity are efficiently utilised at each stage of the process. By

setting clear WIP limits for different processing areas such as check-in, sorting, loading, and unloading, the system can avoid bottlenecks and prevent overloading at any given stage.

3. Managing Flow: Kanban promotes the smooth and continuous flow of work, and this principle could be applied to baggage handling by ensuring a steady progression of baggage through the system. By employing Kanban signals and real-time tracking, staff can monitor and regulate the flow of baggage, thereby reducing wait times, minimising congestion, and improving overall throughput.

4. Adaptive Responsiveness: Kanban's adaptability makes it well-suited for handling unforeseen changes or disruptions in the baggage handling process. The system can swiftly respond to flight delays, gate changes, or other unexpected events by reallocating resources, reprioritising baggage, and adjusting workflows based on real-time updates reflected through the Kanban signals.

5. Collaborative Improvement: Encouraging cross-departmental collaboration and continuous improvement is another key aspect of Kanban. In the context of baggage handling, this would involve fostering communication and coordination between different teams, such as check-in staff, security personnel, baggage handlers, and airline operators. By

sharing real-time information and leveraging Kanban boards or digital displays, teams can collaborate to address any issues and collectively work towards enhancing the efficiency and reliability of baggage handling operations.

6. Data-Driven Decision Making: Kanban's emphasis on data visibility and analytics could be leveraged to track key performance indicators (KPIs) related to baggage handling, such as processing times, error rates, and on-time delivery. By collecting and analysing this data, the system can identify areas for improvement, make informed decisions, and drive operational enhancements.

Adapting Kanban to baggage handling systems would require careful planning, integration with existing technologies (such as baggage scanning and tracking systems), and ensuring proper training for staff to adopt the new processes. Additionally, compliance with aviation security and safety regulations is paramount, and any changes to the baggage handling system must be validated to ensure they align with stringent security protocols.

Overall, the application of Kanban principles to baggage handling can lead to more efficient and reliable operations, improved resource utilisation, and enhanced customer satisfaction through timely and accurate baggage delivery. By visualising and optimising the flow of baggage, limiting work in progress, fostering collaboration, and enabling adaptive responsiveness, a Kanban-based approach holds the potential to transform baggage handling systems within the aviation industry.

Real-time tracking for baggage using Kanban signals

Implementing real-time tracking for baggage using Kanban signals involves leveraging visual management and digital technology to monitor the movement and status of baggage throughout the handling process. Here's a detailed approach to implementing real-time tracking for baggage using Kanban signals:

1. Digital Kanban Cards: Each piece of baggage is assigned a unique digital Kanban card containing essential information such as destination, flight number, passenger details, and priority status. These digital cards serve as the visual representation of the baggage within the Kanban system. The cards can be accessed and updated through a digital platform accessible to relevant staff members involved in baggage handling.

2. RFID or Barcoding: Integrating RFID (Radio Frequency Identification) tags or barcoding technology with the digital Kanban cards enables

real-time tracking of baggage as it moves through different stages of handling. RFID readers or barcode scanners located at key checkpoints, such as check-in counters, sorting areas, loading bays, and aircraft holds, capture the movement of baggage and update the corresponding Kanban cards instantly.

3. Kanban Board or Dashboard: A centralised digital Kanban board or dashboard provides a real-time visualisation of all baggage items being handled within the system. This digital display reflects the status, location, and progression of each piece of baggage, allowing staff to monitor the overall flow and identify any bottlenecks or delays.

4. Automated Status Updates: As baggage moves through various checkpoints, the RFID or barcode scanning devices automatically update the status of the corresponding Kanban cards in the digital system. For example, when baggage is loaded onto an aircraft, the RFID reader at the loading bay registers the event and updates the Kanban card to reflect its "in-flight" status. This automation ensures that the real-time tracking information is accurate and up to date.

5. Alerts and Notifications: The digital Kanban system can be configured to generate alerts and notifications based on predefined criteria. For instance, if a baggage item deviates from its intended route or experiences an unusually long dwell time at a specific checkpoint, the system can trigger alerts to prompt staff to investigate and take corrective actions.

6. Mobile Access for Field Staff: To facilitate real-time updates and tracking, field staff involved in baggage handling can access the digital Kanban system through mobile devices. This enables them to update the status of baggage on the go, perform additional scans if needed, and communicate any exceptional circumstances or issues directly into the system.

7. Integration with Existing Systems: The real-time tracking system must be seamlessly integrated with existing baggage handling technologies, such as scanning equipment, conveyor systems, and airline databases. This integration ensures that the Kanban signals align with the actual physical movement and handling of baggage within the airport environment.

8. Analytics and Reporting: The digital Kanban system captures valuable data on baggage movement, processing times, and performance metrics. Utilising this data, the system can generate reports and analytics to identify trends, optimise workflows, and drive continuous improvements in baggage handling operations.

9. Training and Change Management: Introducing a real-time tracking system based on Kanban signals necessitates comprehensive training for staff members involved in baggage handling. This training should focus on the new processes, the use of digital Kanban cards, RFID scanning procedures, and the interpretation of real-time tracking information.

10. Regulatory Compliance and Security: Given the critical nature of baggage handling within the aviation industry, the real-time tracking system must adhere to stringent regulatory requirements and security protocols. Any changes to the baggage handling processes, including the adoption of real-time tracking technology, must undergo thorough validation and compliance assessments to ensure seamless integration within the existing security framework.

By implementing real-time tracking for baggage using Kanban signals, airports and airline operators can significantly enhance the visibility, efficiency, and reliability of their baggage handling operations. The combination of visual management principles with digital tracking technology empowers staff to monitor and manage baggage in real time, leading to improved customer service, reduced mishandling, and streamlined operational processes. Additionally, the real-time tracking system provides valuable data insights that can drive continuous improvements and optimisations within the baggage handling ecosystem.

Baggage Handling System successful case studies

Two examples of successful baggage handling systems that have demonstrated efficient operations and customer satisfaction:

1. Incheon International Airport, South Korea:

Incheon International Airport, one of the busiest and largest airports in the world, is renowned for its state-of-the-art baggage handling system. The airport's baggage handling system uses advanced technologies, including automated check-in kiosks, RFID tracking, and a high-speed conveyor system. The airport has implemented a comprehensive real-time tracking system for baggage using RFID technology. Each bag is tagged with an RFID chip, allowing for seamless tracking throughout the handling process.

Incheon's baggage handling system integrates real-time tracking with digital Kanban signals to provide visual management and operational oversight. The digital Kanban system displays the status and location of each baggage item, ensuring efficient flow and timely processing. This real-time visibility enables staff to monitor and manage baggage effectively, mitigating potential delays and ensuring accurate routing to the intended flights.

The implementation of a robust baggage handling system, incorporating real-time tracking and digital Kanban signals, has significantly reduced the incidence of mishandled baggage at Incheon International Airport. This, in turn, has led to enhanced customer satisfaction, as passengers experience fewer instances of lost or delayed baggage. The airport's efficient baggage handling operations have contributed to its reputation for delivering a seamless travel experience, reinforcing its status as a leading global aviation hub.

2. Singapore Changi Airport:

Singapore Changi Airport, consistently ranked among the world's best airports, is known for its exemplary passenger experience and efficient operations. The airport has invested in advanced baggage handling technology to streamline processes and ensure minimal disruptions.

Singapore Changi Airport's baggage handling system incorporates real-time tracking and digital Kanban signals to optimise the flow of baggage through the airport. The implementation of RFID technology enables the real-time tracking of baggage, with each item being assigned a digital Kanban card for visual management.

The airport's centralised control centre utilises a digital dashboard to monitor the movement and status of baggage in real time, enabling proactive management of potential issues and facilitating timely interventions.

The integration of real-time tracking with digital Kanban signals has contributed to Singapore Changi Airport's reputation for operational excellence. The airport has achieved high reliability in baggage handling, with minimal instances of mishandled or misplaced baggage. Passengers benefit from the assurance that their luggage is being efficiently managed and tracked throughout the travel process, enhancing their overall travel experience and contributing to the airport's esteemed reputation.

Both case studies demonstrate the successful implementation of real-time tracking for baggage using Kanban signals, resulting in improved operational efficiency and heightened customer satisfaction. The integration of advanced technologies, visual management principles, and real-time tracking capabilities has enabled these airports to uphold high standards of baggage handling, contributing to their positions as leading global aviation hubs.

Summary

In summary, "Air Traffic Control & Baggage Handling: A Kanban Story" provides a comprehensive and practical guide to leveraging Kanban principles in the context of the aviation industry. The book offers valuable insights, real-world case studies, and best practices for implementing Kanban in air traffic control and baggage handling systems.

Readers will gain a deep understanding of how Kanban can be tailored to suit the unique challenges and requirements of air traffic control and baggage handling, leading to improvements in operational efficiency, on-time performance, and overall customer satisfaction.

By embracing the principles of Kanban and incorporating continuous improvement practices, aviation professionals, airport operators, and airline executives can drive meaningful change and enhance the reliability and efficiency of air traffic control and baggage handling systems in today's dynamic aviation landscape.

Foundations of Scrum Agile
Education

£2.99

App Store

Google Play

Agile Development with DevOps

Agile Project Management: Navigating Pros and Cons of Scrum, Kanban and combining them

Air Traffic Control & Baggage Handling: A Kanban Story

Communication Troubles of a Scrum Team

Disney's FastPass: A Queue Story

Introducing the Douglass Model for Agile Coaches

Kaizen: The Philosophy of Continuous Improvement for Business and Education

Mastering Software Quality Assurance: A Comprehensive Guide

McDonald's: A Kanban Story

Nightclub Entry Token System: A Kanban Story

Pizza Delivery: A Kanban Story

Scrum: Unveiling the Agile Method

Testing SaaS: A Comprehensive Guide to Software Testing for Cloud-Based Applications

The Art of Lean: Production Systems and Marketing Strategies in the modern era

The Board: A day-to-day feel of life on a Kanban team

The Sprint: A day-to-day feel of life on a Scrum team

The Whole Game: Systems Thinking Approach to Invasion Sports

Traffic Light System: A Kanban Story

Air Traffic Control & Baggage Handling: 36
A Kanban Story

www.ingramcontent.com/pod-product-compliance
Lightning Source LLC
LaVergne TN
LVHW051649050326
832903LV00034B/4765